It's Not Magic.
But It Can Be Magical

Improving Your Marriage At Any Stage

James 4:17

William P. Thomas, Sr.

ISBN-13: 978-1539712930

IT'S NOT MAGIC

Praise by Readers of *It's Not Magic*

"William has written a practical and useful guide for a healthy and happy marriage. This book reflects his marriage, possessing little fluff, but loads of fun. They truly live out every page of this book. You would do your marriage a favor if you put these principles and practices into play starting now!"

-Ross Wiseman, Founding Pastor of Momentum Church in Woodstock, GA and Director of the GA Church Multiplication Network, husband of 23 years to Amie

---

"When I picked up this book, I chuckled at the irony and sense of humor God has. I remember some 15 years ago when he thought he was good enough for one of my two younger sisters! I've seen him grow into a man after God's heart AND a man who is madly in love with my little sister. What's more, is I see in my sister's eyes the love she has for him. The words of this book bring you into their relationship as William shares with you the principles that govern a quintessential marriage...the principles I personally see him living out on a daily basis. I assure you, he is not practicing what he preaches per se; rather, he is preaching what he practices. This is a MUST READ for relationships at any stage - you are doing yourself a disservice by not doing so."

Steve Q. Riddick, Businessman, Marketplace Minister, Host of "MoneySmart with Steve Riddick", husband of 16 years to Tonya

---

"Some of us don't learn lessons in time to save what we most cherish, but the wisdom shared in this book proves that some do. I'm grateful for the knowledge my friend has decided to share in order to help others avoid the pitfalls that many have fallen into."

-Ron Walker, Author, Speaker, Entrepreneur, no longer married

"I really loved reading this book. I'm trying to make sure that my husband and I have a strong marriage. The recommendations included don't feel outdated for it is coming from someone whose marriage I am able to relate with."

-Whitney Toussaint, Case Manager for the FDIC, wife of 2 years to Lesedi

---

"The great thing about this book is that William and his wife live what they write in an exciting and refreshing way. Their marriage is clear evidence of his passion to love God first, then following the commands of Christ in loving his wife and family with his whole heart. Reading this book is an honest and transparent look into how and why it works. Enjoy and join in."

-Chuck Mingonet, Retired U.S. Navy Captain and Mentor, husband of 36 years to Sandy

---

"Marriage is not easy, but 'It's Not Magic: But It Can Be Magical' gives practical wisdom on the subject. Reading the concise chapters and using the discussions at the end of each chapter can move couples towards a marriage that glorifies the Lord."

-Laura Lawson, Stay at home mother, wife of 10 years to Matt, a church planter in Burbank, CA

"William has inspired my faith in God and marriage for many years: from our church beginnings to his admirable devotion to his wife. He stood beside me at my wedding, a symbol to my wife and me of the sacred, fulfilling promise of marriage. This book is the divine fruition of the incredible example he and his beautiful wife offer married couples seeking to appreciate the magic that marriage can be."

LaMarre and Amalfi Elder, Lawyers, husband and wife of 3 years

4

"It's Not Magic: But It Can Be Magical" does what many books fail to do, which is marry (no pun intended) concept and practical application. Many books provide great concepts but miss out on an opportunity to show readers how to turn concept into reality. This book is not of those books. Whether challenging commonly-given bad advice or discussing healthy compromise in everyday marital situations, William Thomas challenges readers to place premium value on their spouse and their marriage. Whether read by a newlywed or a seasoned couple, this book provides valuable insight into prioritizing marriage and planning for the long haul. Anyone that is married or plans to marry, should definitely take the time out to read."

-Dereko J. Robertson, Church Planter, Coach, and Consultant, husband of 10 years to Melva

---

"After 10 years of marriage, this book was a great reminder of all the reasons why we have made it to the 10 year mark and how to sail through another 10 years. This is a great re-readable resource to keep your marriage healthy and moving in the right direction."

-Erin Thompson, Staff Culture and Development for Woodstock City Church in Woodstock, GA, wife of 10 years to Mike

---

"I've seen William's life both up close and from a distance. One thing is for sure: this man loves Jesus. His affections for the Lord are evidenced in the way he deeply loves his family. If there's a word that comes to mind, it's INTENTIONALITY. William is highly intentional. He loves and leads his family well. For this reason, I know my wife and I will benefit from his faithfulness."

-Dallas White, Pastoral Assistant to Dr. Johnny M. Hunt, husband of 6 years to Amanda

DEDICATION

This is for you, my sweet bride.

This is for our four children whom I hope have a marriage like ours.

CONTENTS

ACKNOWLEDGMENTS

Thanks to everyone who has contributed to our story, spoke truth over our lives, and is instrumental to the growth of our marriage. Thanks to all who've reviewed, proofread, and made suggestions to this book simply because they were asked.

Thanks especially to my parents, in-laws, and grandparents, David and Rhonda Johnson, Harold and Shonen Thomas, Kenneth and Ann Johnson, and Bill and Arbuna Rice for modeling how to love your spouse, extend forgiveness, and grow as one.

To Kelly, my bride, my champion, my partner in life, writer of chapter 14, and reason for this book. To the mother of my children, breath to my dreams, wind to my spirits. I owe this to you.

INTRODUCTION

I am extremely excited for you. I am flattered you have chosen to grow your marriage by using this text as a catalyst. I am astutely aware that there is no way this book can cover everything to make your marriage stronger, but I am confident that by reading and applying, you will see great gains.

This book is a valuable resource for the never married, the newly married, and the veteran married. Its format, a short chapter, followed by Conversations 2 Consider (C2C) encouraging you to discuss, ask, and act, allows the book to be versatile enough for a personal study, a couples' study, or a group discussion study.

My deepest desire for you in reading this book is that your marriage become the one in your dreams. I hope this book is only a start to discovering or rediscovering the value of your marriage. I look forward to hearing the stories of how this book has benefited many.

Marriage discovers its truest meaning when it understands and mirrors that which God instituted it to be. To explore marriage without looking at the greatest love story ever would do readers and marriages a disservice. It is not the story of Romeo and Juliet, nor is it the story seen on the big screen in the movie *Titanic*.

The greatest love story is found in the 66 books of the Bible. It is the story of a Creator God, who demonstrates His love by sending His Son to redeem His creation. Therefore, any reference to love, without mention of Scripture, is a futile attempt. As we look at the intent and benefits of marriage, the inspired word of God will be used as a significant resource.

The truths and assertions from this text are in line with the words of Scripture. For above all, I want you to know that marriage is God's divine plan allowing us to experience unspeakable joy and fulfillment.

The initial, romantic feelings you've experienced will likely fade away: the butterflies in one's stomach, the lump in one's throat, etc. At some point, the unique qualities that originally attracted you to your spouse will annoy you. You must understand that you aren't less in love when *"they can do no wrong"* becomes *"they can do nothing right."*

There is no magic formula or potion for having an optimum marriage. There are no beans you can plant to make it better - no fancy trick for creating the marriage you want. Nope. Marriage is not magic, but as you take responsibility for your part, it can be magical.

STOP RIGHT HERE

IF YOU ARE ON THE EDGE OF GIVING UP, I AM GLAD YOU FOUND THIS BOOK. BE PATIENT TO READ TO THE END. ONCE FINISHED, FEEL FREE TO CONTACT ME AND I WILL MAKE IT A PRIORITY TO PUT YOU IN TOUCH WITH THOSE EQUIPPED TO ASSIST YOU.

1

MARRIAGE IS EASY

"Marriage is easy", said no one ever who has had a great marriage. A married friend of mine once said that after being married for several years, he knew why Jesus never got married. We both laughed at his joke, though I am sure internally we paused to let that statement sink in.

You see, marriage is hard.

You may be reading this book and are in the initial stages of courtship looking towards marriage, recently engaged, newly married, or going on many years of marriage. This truth has either been expressed to you by a counselor, friend, pastor, or parent. Perhaps you and your spouse have discovered this in your own marriage. While we recognize the validity of the difficulties of marriage, it is important to explore why this is. The best place to begin is to look at the first union of man and woman.

In Genesis chapter 1, God creates man and woman, and puts them together in the garden. He creates them in His image, giving them the ability to reason, feel, and commune with one another. He gives them the tasks of being fruitful and having dominion over the rest of His creation.

As you read the account of man's beginning, a key passage of scripture can be read over rather quickly if you are not careful. Genesis 2:16 says, "*The Lord God said, 'It is not good for the man to be alone. I will make a helper suitable for him.*"[1] God knew man would long to have a horizontal relationship along with the vertical one between Him and man. In His sovereignty, He created woman as the ideal (and suitable) partner for him.

Yet despite the perfect union God created, Adam and Eve found themselves separated from God, as a result of their disobedience to His commands. This separation from the perfect unity of God likewise produced a divide in Adam's relationship with Eve, causing their union to experience strife, anxiety, shame, and difficulty. As direct descendants of Adam and Eve, each one of us

---

[1] Unless otherwise noted, all scripture quotations are taken from the NIV.

now bears the weight of their decision and subsequently we find ourselves experiencing the difficulties of marriage.

When my wife and I started dating, we used to play a virtual reality computer game. Each player was responsible for creating characters, helping them find social networks, jobs, happiness and the path towards achieving their aspirations. Some of the fictional characters wanted big homes, others wanted lots of friends; some wanted lots of children and some wanted to fill their homes with big ticket expenditures.

The overarching goal of the game was to become the most popular and amass as much money as possible to purchase the most material possessions. However, I did not want to take the time and put in the work of making friends slowly, work my way up the corporate ladder, or save for a big house. Instead, I learned the cheat code for accessing unlimited money. This enabled me to build the biggest house, even without a job. The cheat code afforded me the opportunity to buy the most expensive paintings, even though I had no income. If I needed more money, I would just type in my cheat code and get some more.

After a while, I lost interest in having nothing else to spend all the money on. Eventually, I stopped playing the game, but not before learning a valuable lesson. I discovered the concept of success being a journey rather than a destination. What made the game fun was working and temporarily struggling, being disappointed about not getting the promotion or raise, losing the job because I made a mistake, etc. What made the game worthwhile was that it was difficult.

A part of marriage is a lot like this game. My marriage is fulfilling as a result of us making our way through difficult times together. Whether it's been financial challenges, trust issues, conception struggles, complacency, misinterpreted expectations, or broken promises, marriage is richer when two people experience the joy on the other end of the diligent work.

If you are reading this chapter, you're likely thinking one of two things:

1. My marriage won't be like yours. It won't be that difficult.
2. If marriage *is* so hard, why bother?

Well, you're right. Your marriage won't be like mine - in fact, it won't be like anyone else's marriage:

- It won't be like that marriage you saw fall apart at the first sign of trouble

- It won't be like the marriage you observed that ended after the kids left the house
- It won't be like the marriage you noticed that only has one partner engaged

It won't be like any of the marriages (good or bad) you've observed because it will be uniquely yours. You can choose to make the good choices of the marriages you've seen that have thrived or you can be one to make the bad choices of the marriages you've seen that haven't survived. It is entirely up to you and your spouse.

This is also the answer to the one who asks "why bother?" Bother because though you know your marriage will require hard work, you are willing to do it. Bother because your marriage will help other couples. Bother because you know your marriage will be worth it *because of* the effort you invest in it.

Building a great marriage is like planting a garden. The work of cultivating the soil, planting the seeds, watering daily, removing the weeds, and keeping critters away is a continuous work. This task seems even more difficult because most of your labor does not yield visual results for a significant period.

It may even seem like there is no reward for your work. Yet, in time, the fruit of your labor will be evident. Scripture teaches that a person's yielded results are based on how that person sows. In 2nd Corinthians 9:6, the Bible instructs, *"Remember this: whoever sows sparingly, reaps sparingly, and whoever sows generously, reaps generously."*

What kind of marriage do you want to have? Rather, are you sowing sparingly in your marriage or generously?

Conversations 2 Consider (C2C): Discuss-Ask-Act

1) Discuss preconceived notions you had coming into marriage.

2) What fears do you have about marriage?

3) Talk about how you will handle difficulties when they arise.

2

THE MYTH OF 50/50

My wife and I met way before Snapchat and Twitter existed. Way before there was Facebook or even Myspace. We met during the days of AOL Instant Messenger and home telephones. Initially, the extent of our conversations were over the phone and we conversed for what seemed like hours at a time.

When I finally got the courage to ask her out, we began what would be one of the greatest love stories ever (sort of biased I'm sure). It has not been all roses and rubies, but it has been real. Early on in our courtship, I would have to admit that I wasn't the knight in shining armor by any stretch of the imagination. I was not even any kind of pauper or jest in the royal party.

I was a 17-year-old, dopy and scrawny looking little kid. Though I did well in school, I had no intentions of going to college

20

right away. I was a young man with no vehicle, a very part time job, bouncing from home to home attempting to finish high school. Honestly, I am uncertain as to what she saw in me.

Every weekend, my then girlfriend and now wife, Kelly, would drive an hour to pick me up from school and another hour to drop me off at her grandmother's house. We would spend Friday and all of Saturday nearly inseparable. Then after church on Sunday, she would make the hour drive once more to drop me off, only to again drive the hour back home.

She continued this pattern from the end of February until the beginning of June. So for 13 weeks, Kelly spent a significant amount of money to drive 250 miles each weekend to see me, simply to make sure that we spent time together. To express the truth a little clearer, I quit my low-paying job because I spent my weekends with her. So, Kelly also bore the financial burden of gas, meals, dates, etc.

She never once complained or threw it in my face. I learned a very vital lesson from my wife even before we were married: our relationship was not about meeting in the middle or keeping track of who did what. It was to be one where maximum effort was exhibited at all times, even if the other did not do their part.

There is a phrase often used and quoted by many well-intentioned individuals. It sounds, at surface level, as if it should be true. This quip has become so cliché that I've heard and read it as advice for struggling couples. That statement:

"Marriage is 50/50"

It makes me cringe every time I hear it. Don't get me wrong. I don't fault those who say this as I am sure they truly do not grasp the gravity of this statement. What they are suggesting is that both partners should meet halfway. They are attempting to infer that marriage cannot work without the effort, help, cooperation, and desire of both partners. It is said with such good intentions that it is a shame it creates an even larger problem.

Truth be told, a 50/50 marriage leaves either one or both partners feeling like they are being short changed as they find themselves doing all the heavy lifting. They become disillusioned and critical with the person they promised to sacrifice for in their vows.

Let's start with a vow that everyone remembers: 'in sickness and in health.' Well in health, both partners can equally work if desired, allowing both the ability to provide for the household. Both can contribute as may have been the expectation during the courtship. But what happens in sickness? What happens if one can

22

no longer give what was expected? Didn't we promise that we would be willing to go beyond meeting in the middle?

Or 'for richer, for poorer.' The same concept is here. If marriage is 50/50, then we ought to have said so in our vows. Instead, I am sure most reading this text have already committed to going beyond this "meeting in the middle" mentality.

Could you imagine if this thought process was evident in school systems with teachers and students alike only expecting a 50/50 relationship? We would have kids failing to give their full effort or attention and teachers only willing to help the ones who seemed to perform up to the teacher's expectations.

Students would become skeptical of the entire process of formal education and teachers would begin to believe that only certain students could learn and succeed. As less people believe in the institution's value, we would begin to see less people embarking on the journey or finding alternative ways to redefine education or its worth.

Can you see how a marriage that is defined by 50/50 particularly, contributes to why so many are seeing diminished value in and are finding ways to redefine its worth?

23

So if you really thought about it, do you want a 50/50 marriage? A marriage where both partners look to meet in the middle, without giving any extra effort to go further? I didn't think so.

Marriage is about two individuals who give 100/100.

You cannot allow yourself to only give half the effort or simply do just enough to get by. No, marriage is supposed to involve two individuals who have committed to walk through life together each giving 100% effort. It doesn't mean that you won't at times meet in the middle; it doesn't mean compromise won't be required at times; it likewise doesn't mean you won't have to push beyond your comfort zone. It simply means that you are committed to giving all you are to ensure the prosperity of this marriage.

By no means am I implying that my wife and I have the perfect marriage that has been devoid of disagreements and arguments. There are times where we certainly don't see eye to eye. However, we have worked diligently to give 100% effort.

A marriage defined by 100% effort from both spouses results in a marriage where no circumstance is too large to be overcome. 100% effort in our marriage has created a bond of unity, allowing us to be open and honest with each other. Though this has not been accomplished overnight, each day builds upon the previous.

Conversations 2 Consider (C2C): Discuss-Ask-Act

1) Discuss the myths or misnomers you have heard coming into marriage.

2) How would you feel if your spouse was not giving 100% effort to the marriage?

3) Talk about a marriage that most shaped your view growing up.

3

DON'T LISTEN: UNLESS THEY HAVE IT

I assume you have been to the dentist at some point in your life. If you went to your dentist's office and noticed the staff's oral hygiene was not up to your standards, wouldn't you find it a bit off putting? If you went in to meet the actual dentist and discovered they allowed their oral care to fall by the wayside, you would not only leave their practice, but you wouldn't take any advice they had given you either, right?

A family member of mine is very conscious about his health. He monitors what he puts in his body, spends time planning his meals, and commits to exercising daily. When I want to adjust my diet or am fighting to get past a physical plateau, his advice is extremely valuable. When he tells me what I am doing wrong, or suggests that I alter my routine, his voice is greatly comforting and also is one that can be trusted.

It is wise to listen because he models what I hope to achieve, therefore earning the right to speak into my life. So why listen to people giving advice about marriage when they don't have the type of marriage you desire?

Why listen to a couple who is not themselves working towards an exemplary marriage - one who has not modeled the quintessential marriage you long for?

This makes no sense - yet, it happens all the time. I've seen partners from troubled marriages seek wisdom from others whose marriage is failing.

Kelly and I consider it a privilege to call ourselves stubborn. Yes, I consider our stubbornness a privilege. Before we were married, there were those who told us we needed to wait. I mean, as teenagers, how could we possibly understand what we were getting into? Even early on in our marriage, there were those who suggested it might be easier if we just gave up and moved on.

Yet, we were too bull-headed to listen. Our mind was always clear: our marriage will last because others' marriages will one-day count on ours. We knew our marriage's purpose, even though there were times of difficulty.

The words of Solomon in Proverbs 12:18 reads, *"Reckless words pierce like a sword, but the tongue of the wise brings healing."* Listen to those who speak wisdom and desire healing in time of struggle. Those whose advice is reckless and concerned with pleasure bring nothing but calamity.

"You're right, you deserve to be happy." "It's ok, at least you tried." "You can only hope to change them so much." "They weren't right for you anyway." "Sometimes love isn't enough." "Not everyone finds their soulmate the first time." These are some of the things that others might say. Think I'm kidding? I am not. I have heard it all coming from the mouths of people who have no right to be doling out advice on marriage.

So let's walk through these bad pieces of advice.

1) "You're right, you deserve to be happy."

Maybe it's because I said my vows so many years ago, but I just cannot recall for the life of me promising that I was only in it as long as I was happy.

2) "It's ok, at least you tried."

The word "try" implies that one has attempted, but has given up. Marriage is not something to be tried nor attempted, instead it is to be committed to.

3) "You can only hope to change them so much."

I hope my wife isn't holding her breath waiting on me to change. Change is not a goal. It is a result of growing. It does not happen simply because someone else desires it.

4) "They weren't right for you anyway."

What does that mean? What is right? If you didn't think this when your relationship progressed from dating to engaged, or subsequently from engagement to marriage, why do you think they aren't right now?

5) "Sometimes love isn't enough."

Love was not the only reason you married in the first place, I hope. You got married because you believed in the other person. You trusted them. You dreamed about your life together. You enjoyed them. I have to believe that love wasn't the only reason why you were wed.

6) "Not everyone finds their soulmate the first time."

If you can give me a meaning of the word 'soulmate', without it differing from anyone else's definition, then I'll give you a pass. Therein lies the dilemma. Each definition, which will differ, leads me to believe that there is no such thing as a soulmate.

Any advice like this, coming from someone who does not have the marriage you desire, should have no say regarding your marriage. Stop letting those people lease the space in your head.

Conversations 2 Consider (C2C): Discuss-Ask-Act

1) Discuss bad pieces of advice you have received.

2) Are you aware of any in your life whose opinion you should ignore?

3) Write down the bad advice you've heard and detail how you will combat it together.

4

TIME, TIME OUT, TIME'S UP

Time

I read a book, *The Five Love Languages* by Gary Chapman, several years ago that provided some great insight into how I am to love my wife.[2] That book, in part, is one of many reasons I decided to produce this text. It was concise and short, yet practical. I learned several things by reading that book that I wanted to build upon. I learned that what I wanted from my wife was not the same thing she wanted from me. How I showed Kelly I loved her had more to do with how I wanted to be loved, than how she wanted to be loved.

---

[2] Gary Chapman, *The 5 Love Languages,* (Chicago, IL: Northfield Publishing, 1995).

I discovered that while I longed to be told how much I was appreciated and needed, Kelly did not need to be affirmed as much. While it is always a good practice to tell your spouse how much you value them and desire them, I found out that my wife, more than anything else, longed for me to simply just spend time with her.

Looking at the life of Jesus, we find the greatest example of the importance of spending time with the one we love and cherish. In Luke 6:12, it records Jesus getting away to spend all night with God. By doing so, Jesus modeled two things for us. First, He demonstrated how we ought to spend time with our Heavenly Father. Second, He provided a template for why we are to spend time with our spouse.

Relationships, especially marriages, need time to grow closer. The more I paid attention to my wife, the more I realized our shared need to spend time with one another. With all that has the potential to compete for my attention, i.e. work, school, church, kids, bills, etc., she feels most loved when I set aside the distractions of life and spend time focused on her.

Of all the commodities in the world, time is the only one that is completely unable to be replenished. All other commodities (i.e. money, gas, energy, metals, fuel, water, etc.) can be harvested, harnessed, created, or manufactured over time. But, it is time itself that once gone, can never again be gained.

If you are looking for a first step to bettering your marriage, clear your schedule for an hour soon and spend some time together.

Time Out

Just so you know, I am not implying that you put your spouse in the corner or ground them. I am not suggesting that you take a break from each other. I am simply saying exactly what I wrote: take some time to go out.

Husbands, I know you wish I wouldn't admit this, but we like to get dressed up, wear our new watch, and splash ourselves with our favorite cologne just as much as our wives like to wear that new dress, step into their classy heels, and spray themselves with the perfume they have been saving for a special outing.

Enjoy yourselves. See a movie. Grab a fancy meal. Stay out late. For goodness sakes, just go out!

Do you want to know what happens when you go out? You have a good time together. He can remind you that he is the gentleman you fell in love with and she can show you that she thinks your jokes (that you made up just for her) are still funny. You can be worry free - even if only for a short period of time. You can be reminded that you once were two people willing to do this thing called marriage together, no matter what.

Time's Up

Again, this is not a suggestion nor an endorsement to give up on marriage after a particular time. It is me telling you that it is time to let go of the silly grudge, the petty argument, and the unimportant spat that you had weeks ago.

Don't get me wrong, there will be issues that will shape your marriage more than others. Undoubtedly there will be times where hurt takes longer to dissipate and may never completely. This is not really what I am addressing. It's the little, childish disagreements that I am talking about.

The dish that was left on the counter...the light left on downstairs...the time he/she hogged the remote...the $3 over budget for the groceries. None of these are worth going to bed one night mad or offended, let alone multiple nights. A wise family member of mine has a saying, "*You can't unscramble eggs and you can't unspill milk.*" Sometimes you should just move on.

The time is up on holding a grudge you've held far too long.

Conversations 2 Consider (C2C): Discuss-Ask-Act

1) Talk about your idea of a perfect date.

2) What occupies your time now that could be used for your spouse?

3) Are there any grudges you should give up now? Any forgiveness needed to be extended?

4) Plan time together tomorrow.

5

TAKE OUT THE TRASH AND FILL THE TANK

Tim Keller, a well-respected pastor of a large church in Manhattan and author of a book on marriage, makes a profound statement in the book's intro. He says, *"If God invented marriage, then those who enter it should make every effort to understand and submit to His purposes for it."*[3] Though it appears that marriage is not looked upon as important as it was a generation ago, God's purposes for marriage have not changed.

After the fall of man and subsequent banishment from the garden, Adam and Eve began to feel the consequences of their sin. Adam was punished by receiving a never-ending quest to produce from the ground by the sweat of his labor. Today this translates into man's seemingly insatiable appetite to achieve, advance, and

---

[3] Timothy Keller and Kathy Keller, *The Meaning of Marriage* (New York, Dutton, 2011), 6.

accumulate.   Through man's sin, God took the task of working, which was created to occupy and give pleasure to man, and made it an object by which he struggled and yet still idolized.[4]

Likewise, Eve was saddled with a continual draw for her husband. Her longing for him, though God created it to be equally reciprocated, often is now met with resistance and subordinated under man's need and desire to work.

In spite of God's original design for marriage, we find ourselves competing against our spouses at times. Husbands, in many cases, are straining to gain an advantage in the workplace so that they can provide for their wives. Wives, in those instances, often find themselves longing that their husbands be less concerned with their potential advancement and more attentive to them.

As a husband, I understand that providing for my family is important. However, I have discovered my wife doesn't mind me working hard if I do three things:

1. Spend time with her (which we've discussed);
2. Take out the trash; and
3. Make sure she has gas in the tank when she goes out.

---

[4] Genesis 3.

It's not that my wife is incapable or unwilling to take out trash or fill her tank up with gas. For that matter, it is not my job as a man (per se) to do these things. Rather, they are not tasks my wife would volunteer to do - hence why these things happen to be what my wife needs *me* to do. The exact tasks your spouse needs from you is likely to be different; however, the point still stands.

If you are unaware of what your spouse prefers not to do at this time, or if you are just beginning your journey, let me share with you how I discovered that she preferred to have gas in the tank, rather than to pump it herself.

During the course of running some normal errands alone one day, my wife became aware that the amount of fuel remaining in the vehicle would not get her home. As you know, when car manufacturers make vehicles, one precaution they install on the dashboard is an indicator that lights up and in most vehicles chimes when the gas in the car is nearly gone. After seeing this, she called me and asked a question: "If the light has come on, will I make it home?"

My wife, knowing how far she was away from the house, had little doubt that if she did not stop for gas, she would not make it home. Yet, there was a purpose in calling me. First, it was to let me know that she was accustomed to having gas in the car. Second, it was to make sure I knew that she did not care to be without gas again.

When your spouse doesn't like doing something, it may be obvious even if they fail to say the words.

I promise you, if you are paying attention, you won't miss what your spouse's "thing" is.

It may be clearing the dishes off the counter, even if it's just one cup. It may be cutting the grass before it gets a certain length. It may be washing the laundry before being forced to use the towels out of the kid's laundry closet. It may be changing the light bulbs as soon as they blow out. Whatever it may be, find out what it is and do it.

Let me conclude this chapter with a word of wisdom. When you are reading, please keep the focus on you. Don't begin thinking, "My husband/wife needs to hear this or read this." Do not go and shove this chapter in his or her face. Instead, start praying that your spouse would recognize your areas of need and begin doing those things as God lays it upon their heart.

That said, you better believe, my wife doesn't take out the trash and has gas in the car 99% of the time (leaving room for error here).

Conversations 2 Consider (C2C): Discuss-Ask-Act

1) Tell your spouse something you really don't like doing yourself.

2) For women/wives: Your position above your husband's job should be secure. Discuss how you will keep from making your husband feel like he must choose.

3) For men/husbands: While it is understood that you must provide, how will you keep providing from becoming prioritized above your wife?

4) Whatever your spouse told you they did not like to do, do it for them the next time it comes up.

6

LOSING SOMETIMES IS WINNING

The 2016 Summer Olympics in Rio was host to a multitude of great athletic performances and many new world records. Individuals, from several countries, represented their country and did so well.   Despite the many medals given out and accolades earned, there was one instance above all that exemplified what winning truly looks like, even in defeat.

United States distance runner Abbey D'Agostino and New Zealand runner Nikki Hamblin both fell during the 5,000 meter second semifinal heat. Instead of getting up and continuing, the American runner stopped to check on Hamblin.   Then moments later, when she fell, the New Zealand athlete, likewise, stopped.

D'Agostino, having serious injuries to her knee, tearing her ACL and straining her MCL, finished nearly two minutes behind the heat winner. Yet it did not stop those around her, including the commentators, from noting how she stopped to wait on another runner. Though she lost her heat, she won the respect, trust, and admiration of those who ran alongside her.

Some would say that by worrying about another runner, she cost herself a chance to win. I beg to differ! Like this runner, even when you feel like you may have lost, you may have instead won.

There have been times I've lost the discussion regarding money, but I've won my wife's voice. I've lost the conversation over where we live, but I've won my wife's sense of security. I've lost the disagreement on boundaries, but I've won my wife's sense of trust.

I did a search for the most accurate definition of the word "lose". My discovery of the meaning of the word may change how we look at losing. Merriam-Webster's definition is *"to be unable to find or to fail to keep or hold something of value."*[5] In order to lose something, one must be prevented from gaining equal to that which was lost.

---

[5] "Lose," retrieved from http://www.merriam-webster.com/dictionary/lose.

Therefore, where I have "lost" the discussion regarding money, I didn't actually lose any. No money was taken during the discussion, nor was I unable to find the money being discussed. While deciding where to live, my wife didn't choose to live nowhere. We still have a home, a place to lay our heads. When discussing appropriate friendships and relationships, I didn't lose any but instead gained a more appropriate view of subordinating them under my relationship with my wife.

Even if I were to actually experience loss, the question remains:

Wouldn't I much rather lose what's not as important, to win what really is?

We must not forget: husbands and wives are in this together. Marriage is a journey where both are dependent on each other to complete it. Like anything worth working towards, marriage requires a significant investment of time. More specifically, marriage takes perseverance and intentional planning expressed over time.

Perseverance

Romans 5:4 reads, "*Perseverance [produces] character, and character [produces] hope.*" Paul is helping us to see there is a benefit to pressing on as perseverance produces character, which in turn produces hope. This principle is applicable when it comes to dieting, working out, finishing college, learning to ride a bike, or house breaking a pet. Each of the tasks require that one continue to remain steadfast and resolute to see the challenge through to completion. Each builds character and operates in the hope that one day, what you began, will result in attaining the goal you set out for.

Marriage is worthy of each individual's commitment to persevere. Both partners grow in their character as they learn to seek the best for the other spouse. They learn to place their needs after their spouse's need at times. Thus, perseverance culminates in hope and belief. Both hope in the continued growth of their marriage and believe in the efforts of the other.

Intentional Planning

"You must inspect, what you expect." I used to say this a lot when I was in business. It certainly applies to marriage as well. If we desire our marriage to be one of satisfaction, joy, and dually valued, we must begin with a clear, concise expectation. Though it goes against our natural and selfish longing, we must seek out ways to put our spouse's needs and wants above our own.

Set expectations regarding the issues that may come up later on. Discuss how you will handle finances. Consider if, how many, and how you will raise and discipline your children. Talk about what the options are if you are unable to have a traditional family. Explore how you will communicate with each other when tough conversations must happen. Define the boundaries on social engagement. Choose how you will grow spiritually. Make note of the values you both have in common as well as areas that you may not esteem as high.

While starting this practice before marriage is ideal, you may find yourself just approaching the subject of a plan. Yet, it is imperative to grasp that there is no limit to the benefits of taking the time to develop your plan, even years into your marriage.

Conversations 2 Consider (C2C): Discuss-Ask-Act

1) Name one area where you will put your partner's needs above your own.

2) Talk about potential areas where winning may come at the expense of giving up your way.

3) What is more important to you: winning or agreeing?

4) Using the material discussed in the second to last paragraph of this chapter, develop a plan of how you will handle these areas.

7

EVERY DAY CAN BE CHRISTMAS

Do you recall the excitement of waking up Christmas morning as a child? Do you remember how your heart pounded as you leaped to your feet, frantically ran to the living room, and carefully sifted through the wrapped, bowed boxes in pursuit of your gift? Can you still feel your eyes as they widened, slowly scanning around the tree, as you looked for the biggest and best gift with your name on it? Do you remember the emotion that came when you found it? How excited you were and how special you felt that someone would take the time to get you this gift? You felt important, loved, and valued all at once.

This feeling is no different as an adult. Have you ever spent weeks researching, looking for, shopping for, and finally picking up that perfect gift for your spouse? You scoured the internet, the catalogs, or the department stores, hoping to find the exact one.

Once you found it, you brought it home and admired it. Carefully, you wrapped it, making sure the tape and paper covered up everything as to not give away the design on the outer package. You tied the bow once, then took it apart, and tied it a second time, to guarantee that it was perfect. Finally, hiding it in the closet to be revealed at a specific time, you thought about how excited your partner would be when the gift was opened.

When you really think about it, this feeling of excitement was not just about the gift. Instead, it was the anticipation of seeing your spouse's face light up when they opened the gift themselves. You knew when the gift was opened, your spouse would understand the amount of time and energy expended to find this gift and would feel incredibly loved.

Your joy came as a result of you placing an emphasis on the recipient of your gift.

I've learned it is never about a particular day, rather your joy comes as a result of your *choice* to value the recipient on that day.

Marriage can be full of this same feeling, too. There should be a pure excitement of waking up with the person you have committed, chosen, and claimed to spend the rest of your life with.

This is my reality. Every day, I wake up with the pleasure of being married to the woman beside me.

I am ecstatic I get to live life with her, tackle the next challenge, begin the next chapter, build the next bridge, and create a new memory. I feel this way, despite what may have happened the night before, or the week previous. I feel this way even in conflict or in disagreement. At times, the conflict makes me cherish our life together even more. Despite any dispute we may have, Kelly is willing to work through it. In conflict, as we discussed last chapter, we build perseverance, which again leads to character and hope.

It can be just like Christmas morning. You may have gone to bed mad at your parents for not letting you catch Santa or get that last sip of eggnog. But all of that will be gone when you wake up the next morning. Why? It's because the next day is Christmas.

If we are truthful, there is nothing inherently special about December 25th, except that an emphasis has been put on it. If there was no emphasis, it would be like any other day. What I've come to understand, is that it's not the gift that matters. It's not even that day that is important. What matters is the *emphasis* we put on this day that makes us so excited. We choose to be excited although we are not sure what is to come.

No greater could this choice be obvious than in scripture. In Psalms 118:24, the writer reveals this truth when he writes, *"Today is the day that the Lord has made, I will be glad and rejoice in it."* Notice we don't find the writer saying he will rejoice when he discovers what the day holds or when he finds out if the day concluded with a personal benefit.

Rejoicing in that day is a direct result of one thing and one thing only: that day was one the Lord made. This truth confirms we have a choice in the matter and must make the decision beforehand. This choice is the same in our marriages. We can place an emphasis on each day, choosing to wake up excited. Every day of our marriage can be like Christmas, if we make it that way.

Conversations 2 Consider (C2C): Discuss-Ask-Act

1) Take turns describing what "everyday Christmas" would look like.

2) In times of conflict, would you rather discuss right away, after emotions have settled, or not at all?

3) Commit to starting each day fresh.

8

SOCIAL MEDIA'S PLACE

I'm certain some readers are grateful to see this title, while others are a little less enthused. Social media is one subject which undoubtedly has sparked some debates among married couples. As I suggested earlier, a discussion on the purpose and boundaries regarding social media is best done before an issue arises, particularly before embarking upon the journey of marriage.

First, let me clearly articulate that social media will not hide your fallacies, but instead highlights the areas you struggle with. If you struggle with lust or pride, distrust or jealousy, discontentment or a lack of restraint, social media is not going to mask it. Instead it will only magnify those struggles. However, it is with confidence that I can proclaim that I have allowed social media's presence to improve my marriage, and am certain, that if you allow, can do the same for you also.

Let me take the time to articulate my reasoning for saying this.

There is nothing inherently bad about social media. It is a great vehicle to connect with family and friends. It allows people to keep in contact with others despite geographical distances. Information can travel through this medium with a lightning speed that could not happen any other way.

Many great causes and crusades are generated from social media. Injustices are discussed. Views are shared. Thoughts are expressed. Regarding the many purposes of social media, I can say nothing critical. However, what I can criticize is how it is used.

That said, let me lead with this statement about my marriage: social media's presence has made my relationship with my wife better. It has improved my marriage because it has opened another line of communication between us. Reading stories on various platforms has allowed us to express some emotions, at times, that we may have otherwise not explored. We've cried watching videos, chuckled internally reading posts, become angry witnessing the treatment of some, empathized with others, and rolled on the floor laughing over a countless number of things.

However, social media can create damage when one or both partners begin seeing it as a way of escape or a way to alleviate their discontentment. Let me say this clearly:

Social media doesn't make the problem in one's marriage, but it certainly amplifies it.

Exodus 20:17 commands that we are not to covet, or yearn for another's possessions. If allowed, social media will compete for our satisfaction. It can become an idol, removing God out of His rightful place and easily marginalizing our spouse's value. If you find yourself running to social media, for approval or validation, at the slightest annoyance or smallest sign of disagreement, it is time to rethink your presence on that platform.

Instead, allow social media to become another avenue in which you build your spouse up. Seeing a virtual note left by my wife conveying to me how valuable I am (whether in a private forum or public) is an instant brightener to any gloomy day. I am almost certain the feeling is mutual for her, as well.

Use social media as a way to open conversations that may be difficult to bring up otherwise. Take advantage of the connections and resources that may become available through the various platforms. Allow it to be the place where other marriages are encouraged and lifted up by seeing yours.

Kelly and I have never apologized for sharing our lives with others through social media. Though our intent and purpose is not to be applauded by others, we have received many private messages, texts, emails, and calls encouraging us to continue to be a light to others through our marriage.

It does not mean that at times, our marriages will not experience rough times. On the contrary, I am 100% positive we all will occasionally experience rough patches in our marriages. However, Kelly and I choose to work on these privately while allowing others to share in the victory we seek to live in.

Conversations 2 Consider (C2C): Discuss-Ask-Act

1) Discuss what you would find inappropriate if your spouse was hiding it from you.

2) What would others say about your marriage based on your social media presence?

3) Tell your spouse what you plan to use social media for.

9

REMEMBER YOUR VOWS

According to the CDC and the National Survey of Family, there are over 2,000,000 marriages in the United States yearly.[6] Despite the abundance of data that hints to the difficulties of marriage, this does not prevent over 4,000,000 men and woman from joining together every year. What then, is this draw in us towards marriage? Why do we long to spend our lives, forever, with another individual? Is there something inside of us that craves this union?

In the 2nd chapter of Genesis, the writer states that man and woman will leave their mother and father, and cling to their spouse. In Ephesians 5:32, Paul echoes the Genesis statement and follows it by saying, *"This mystery is profound."* It surely is! The mystery of

---

[6] "STATS | Marriage Statistics - Statistic Brain", Statistic Brain, last modified 2016, accessed September 5, 2016, http://www.statisticbrain.com/marriage-statistics.

marriage is unexplainable except to suggest that God created us with a natural yearning to be committed to another.

Though these may not be the exact words you repeated, most marriage vows contained the following components.

"I [Input your name], take [Input your spouse's name], from this day forward, to have and to hold, for better, for worse, for richer, for poorer, in sickness and in health, to love and to cherish, forsaking all others, till death us do part."

If you said something like this, nod your head in agreement. When you said the words, you meant them, right? Nod again. Then, it is imperative that we live out our marriages as if we meant the vows we said.

Let's break down these vows and walk through what we said and hopefully what we meant.

I [Input your name] - Yes, you, me, myself, I, chose this. No one else did, but you and me.

Take [Input your spouse's name] - No one else is making this commitment with you. You did not promise to take anyone besides the one whose name you've said.

From this day forward - Beginning today. There is no retreat, nor surrender.

To have and to hold - You are responsible for the care and wellbeing of the one whom you've committed to.

For better, for worse - This covers anything you could possibly think of or say to get out of this commitment.

For richer or poorer - Bank account balance and/or income level does not dictate the quality or success of your marriage.

In sickness and in health - You committed to being there even when age or health alter your reality.

To love and to cherish - The privilege of loving our spouse is having the ability to value and hold them in high esteem also. What a joy this is!

Forsaking all others - We promise to forsake anyone that is not who we committed to.

Till death us do part - It doesn't end before this, but don't get any bright ideas.

When we said these words, we said them in front of our friends and family. While everyone was watching, we repeated the words of the minister or rabbi or priest. More importantly, we proclaimed these vows before God, our Heavenly Father. At the conclusion of proclaiming these vows before Him, the officiator of the ceremony confirmed this vow with the words of Mark 10:9, *"What God has joined together, let no man separate."*

It is this pronouncement that binds together the words the husband and wife have just said. There should be nothing and no one (including ourselves) that can separate us. If it takes you re-reading this chapter, or reviewing your wedding covenant vows, every time you find yourself in a struggle, then visit them often. Your marriage is worth it to both partners and to God who created it.

Conversations 2 Consider (C2C): Discuss-Ask-Act

1) Discuss which vow has been most difficult to accept/live out.

2) Have you kept each vow you said at your wedding?

3) Standing face-to-face, repeat your vows to each other.

10

MAKE SMALL BETS

Unless you have no shame and were confident in yourself, there were things you refused to do around your boyfriend/girlfriend while you were dating. Likewise, there were things you did simply because you were in the giddy, flirty stage. While they may be classified as corny or cheesy, you did them because you placed an emphasis on keeping your relationship fresh and entertaining.

During the eight months of dating, prior to us marrying, you couldn't get Kelly and me off the phone with each other. Even if we had just left each other or spent the entire weekend together, the moment we were separated, we would jump on our phones, calling the other just to hear their voice.

I am sure most of our conversations were spent laughing at each other, nervously plotting out our lives together, making up the craziest names for our kids, and planning the wildest trips we would take after we were married. Yet, it never failed that eventually the time would come to say our goodbyes. This time would always bring out the most competitive sides of both of us. Neither would want to be the first to get off the phone, each trying to be the last to say they loved the other.

It is safe to say, that because of our competitive nature, this chapter made it in this book. It may not even be a help to most marriages. Nevertheless, since it has helped mine, I feel obligated to share it.

At least once a week, my wife and I will have different recollections of events or dissimilar conclusions about verifiable facts. I've said before, *"if only we got that on tape"*, to which my wife would reply, *"Yeah, me too, so I could prove you wrong."* The invention of Google and the video record feature on mobile devices has cleared up many cases where we didn't see eye to eye.

When this happens, it doesn't take long before one of us will suggest that we agree upon a friendly wager. After defining the rules, we set a time frame for repayment. Normally, our favorite wager is a 5-minute massage to be given by the loser upon demand. But we've wagered dinner, small cash, and pride, among other things.

The great thing about these small bets is that they allow us to keep our marriage fresh. We have so much fun together through the disagreement, anticipating the other being wrong, and then discovering the answer. Find what it is that keeps your marriage moving ahead. It could be the little bets. It could be cooking the new meals together. It may be recreating past dates. Whatever it is, discover it and do it often.

Understand that the point of this chapter is not to compete with your spouse. Remember, you are together in this thing. It is, however, written as a way of encouraging you to find ways to grow closer. Though these small bets seemingly pit one spouse against another, it has done the exact opposite in our marriage and instead brought us closer together.

I asked a man recently, who has been married to his wife for 54 years, what he thought about this concept. He said that this very thing has been a critical part of his marriage. He realized that in losing a bet, he found ways to prioritize his wife over himself.

Though I wish I could say to the contrary, I've given out significantly more massages than I have received. But this is one of those cases where losing is really winning. I lost the bet, but my wife got a much needed massage. I lost the bet, but my wife got the quality time she needed from me. I lost the bet, but the massage turned into...I'll encourage you to use your imagination here. I've won, even when I've lost.

Conversations 2 Consider (C2C): Discuss-Ask-Act

1) Talk about ways to keep your marriage fresh.

2) Do you believe that it is common for spouses to compete with one another? Why or why not?

3) Bet a 5-minute massage the next time you disagree on something provable.

11

ONCE A MONTH

Cast iron. Judgment. Slippers. Jeans. Leather boots. Decision making. What do all these things have in common? Each is considered to get better as time goes on. Shouldn't this assertion be true also of our marriages? Dustin Heiner states, in the very first paragraph of his book, Lasting Marriage: Discovering God's Meaning and Purpose for Your Relationship, that as marriage is established to be a lifelong union, it should *"get better and more enjoyable the longer you are married."*[7]

As your marriage crosses over into each passing year, it should hope to be better than the year before. You should know your spouse more, trust them a little more, and enjoy them even more than years prior. But how can we be certain this happens?

---

[7] Dustin Heiner and Melissa Heiner, *Lasting Marriage: Discovering God's Meaning and Purpose for Your Relationship* (Triune Publishers, 2016), 9.

Look again at the items mentioned above. What else do they have in common? Each gets better with time in direct proportion to the use they receive.

One identifiable way to monitor "use" in a marriage is to track the time you spend dating your spouse.

Unfortunately, after the honeymoon stage, many couples stop dating. The rationale develops unconsciously. They internally assume that they have arrived at the culmination of their lives together and dating is no longer a necessary task. This particularly rings true as life gets busy with jobs, graduate school, yard work, and children. However, this is neither an accurate view nor an acceptable one. Randy Southern, in his book, 62 Uncommon Dates, goes as far as to say that *"dating is to marriage what breathing is to the body."*[8]

Putting a scheduled date night on the calendar lets your spouse know that they are valued and important. It creates an anticipation of getting away and getting alone. Married folks need to get out of the house at least once a month. In Chapter 17, I will

---

[8] Randy Southern, *52 Uncommon Dates: A Couples Adventure Guide for Praying, Playing, and Staying Together* (Chicago, IL: Moody Publishers, 2014), 7.

share some ideas of what you can do, but I'll let you in on one thing that we've done that has helped significantly in this area.

Last year, entering our 14th year of marriage, my wife suggested that every month, on the 14th, we go out to commemorate the year. So for all that year, we went out on the 14th, doing things that we had never tried before or visiting places we had never visited. Some were a bit out of the other's comfort zone and there were some we discovered that we loved.

A month after completing our 15th year of marriage finds us still going out at least once a month. Simply by making continual dating a part of our lives, we have added 22 dates over the past 22 months, and have no intentions of stopping.

An obvious dilemma comes when we get past the 28th year, for the month of February, the 30th, for half of the months, and then the 31st year for the rest. Well, this works out to our advantage and is a simple solution to us. Taking two days of the month equal to that year of marriage, we gain an extra date night. For example, in year 32, we may go out on the 7th and the 25th.

That means, if the Lord wills, should we experience another 50 years of marriage (feasible since we got married as teenagers) we will have added a total of 1,072 dates after our 15th year of marriage. I don't apologize for saying that this is purely amazing.

Though you may be already in your 15th year, or your 20th, or even your 50th, you can start now. Imagine the newlywed or even the newly engaged implementing this in their relationship. Imagine how many more dates they will experience in their lives if they begin emulating this practice right now. It excites me more than you know to even think about it.

Conversations 2 Consider (C2C): Discuss-Ask-Act

1) Count how many times you have been on a date in the past year.

2) What date is the most memorable and why?

3) Schedule a monthly date for at least the next 6 months, even if you don't completely know your schedule yet.

4) Email me and tell me you planned your date and feel free to share details of your plan, if you would like. (I've included my email at the end of the book).

12

LAUGH AND DON'T STOP

Growing up, my grandparents' marriage was the one that I looked to and hoped to one day model. Being the ever inquisitive kid (or nosey, as the grown-ups called it) I wondered how they met and started dating. Though I never had the courage to ask as a child, I took the liberty recently on a visit home and asked my grandfather.

Like many young men of the 1950's, my grandfather sung in a quartet. Being on the stage was a natural thing for him and it certainly made him a heartthrob for the young women. But, there was one pretty lady in particular, one whom he asked his friends about and inquired of her friends about.

As he began to tell me the story of how they began to court, I was certain that he was embellishing a bit. However, my grandmother just sat there smiling and nodding along. So I continued to listen as he told the story of when they were married and how he opened his record store and how they bought their first house.

Sitting back, resting in the memories he had just relived, my grandmother just couldn't contain herself anymore. She let out a grand laugh and said, *"Bill, are you done with telling that exaggeration?"* Quickly looking back at my grandfather, waiting for him to respond, I noticed he had "dozed off" with a smile on his face. 60 years later and they still know how to laugh together.

I know that my Kelly at least gives the illusion that she finds me funny. Sometimes though, I am not sure if she is laughing at me, with me, because of me, in spite of me, or in some cases, variations of all of the above. Regardless, I do know that she laughs and I laugh with her. Just recently, while walking, I tripped over what appeared to be ground that rose up simply for the purpose of tripping me, and then mysteriously receded back into place. Of course, she had to let me know she saw this by chuckling out loud.

Thankfully, within the hour, the same thing happened to her. If you are wondering if I took the high road, go back, and reread the title of this chapter. I reminded her, not only by laughing, but by chiding her for tripping over air. But guess what? We were laughing. I am even proud to say, that I am slightly smiling as I write these very words.

The Mayo Clinic published an article noting that laughter, among many other benefits, soothes tension, removes pain, increases personal satisfaction, and improves one's mood.[9] Tell me we can't use all of these. What marriage doesn't need, from time to time, tension soothed, hurtful experiences momentarily forgotten, increased contentment, and a jolt to alter a grumpy mood? Laughter does all of these things.

Laughter can come from the random, the planned, the forced, and the unexpected.

Figure out what makes your partner laugh and do it often, even at the expense of yourself. Look for ways and situations to facilitate laughter. Go dancing or surfing and I promise you'll be laughing sooner than later.

---

[9] Mayo Clinic Staff, "Stress Relief From Laughter? It's No Joke," *Mayo Clinic,* http://www.mayoclinic.org/healthy-lifestyle/stress-management/in-depth/stress-relief/art-20044456?pg=2, April 21, 2016.

I am certain that the primary beneficiary of laughter within marriage is the person who causes their spouse to laugh. Laughter relays to our spouse that we are completely at ease, even if for a moment.

We are not focusing on the bills, the kids, work the next morning, the pets, or the fact that we skipped a meal. There's a saying that "*a happy wife equals a happy life.*" Though true, I've found this mantra to be more accurate: A laughing spouse equals a loving house.

Conversations 2 Consider (C2C): Discuss-Ask-Act

1) Talk about a time that your spouse made you laugh.

2) Think about how you feel when you are laughing compared to when you aren't. How does it make you feel?

3) Find a marriage that you respect and ask them to share the story of how they met.

13

TOO SHORT TO BE MISERABLE…AND TOO LONG

I honestly can't believe it has been 15 years already. I remember the day like it was yesterday. Standing there in front of the judge, in my blue jeans and white T-shirt. Whiskers barely on my top lip, I gazed at my bride-to-be, who too was trembling, yet composed and beautiful. There we made our vows before our family and slipped the rings over our skinny fingers. Our eyes were bright and our aspirations were high as we anticipated life together – yet we were oblivious to what it all really meant. It seems like yesterday.

Yet, in the same thought it seems like forever ago. Forever ago that we weren't concerned about tomorrow or the next day, released from the arguments that lasted too long, and free from the self-imposed shackles of anger or disappointment regarding life as we knew it at times. Sometimes hours seemed like days, and days seemed like years, although those hours and days were very rare.

Considering that, here's a truth I want to sink in. Marriage is way too short. It will go way too fast to look back at it and to discover that you were miserable. Don't allow yourself to look back and realize you wasted valuable time with your spouse. Even if you find this is a present reality, begin today anew, choosing not to be miserable.

That said, however, don't forget the second part of this truth either. Marriage is way too long. It will seem way too slow to be in a continual state of misery. You committed to be with this person for the rest of your life, so why be miserable? You have a choice in the matter.

During my research, one problem continued to claim responsibility for a significant amount of misery amongst couples. The men, in many cases, felt most miserable when they believed they were not being respected by their wives. Similarly, the wives experienced much of their misery when they did not feel loved by their husbands. Thankfully, scripture addresses both concerns in Ephesians 5.

Ephesians 5:22-33 asserts that wives are to submit to their husbands. I am aware that this is the passage some husbands were hoping I would get to and some wives were just waiting for me to bring up as an excuse to put this book down. Before either party jumps to conclusions, hear me out.

Men, the writer is not inferring that this is a license to rule and dominate our wives.

Women, this is not a suggestion that you are to sit back in silence. Instead, it is encouraging men to take on the challenge of leading in every area. It is an admonishment to make wise decisions, rather than irrational ones. It is a reminder that we are now responsible for the wife we have committed to.

When the author suggests later that husbands are to love their wives, he is not saying that this is to be done only as the wife is showing honor and submission towards her husband. The command is not dependent on the wife submitting to her husband.

Wives, consider it a privilege to submit to your husbands and trust their leadership. Submit so they know you trust their choices. Husbands, love your wives so that they can trust your choices. Love them so they want to submit themselves to your leadership. I love that my wife submits to my leadership. I love it just as much, if not more, that she feels secure enough to challenge my viewpoint in the hopes of helping me to see other perspectives when I need to. I love that she never fails to live up to her responsibility in Ephesians 5, even when I fail in mine.

With all the talk about love in the previous paragraphs, it begs the question, what really is love? In his book *Boundaries in Marriage,* Dr. Henry Cloud notes that many of us have no stronger yearning than to enjoy a lifetime of love and commitment to one individual. He goes on to say that love is being bound together in such a way as to overcome hurt, a lack of maturity, and self-centeredness to produce something better together than alone.[10]

Love is a vital component of marriage. Love is necessary to sustain and grow a marriage. However, too many simply write love off as just a feeling, without truly grasping what all it means. The Apostle Paul specifically addressed the concept of love in his first letter to the church located in Corinth. In chapter 13 of 1st Corinthians, Paul wrote, *"Love is patient, love is kind. It does not envy, it does not boast, it is not proud. It does not dishonor others, it is not self-seeking, it is not easily angered, it keeps no record of wrongs. Love does not delight in evil but rejoices with the truth. It*

---

[10] Henry Cloud and John Townsend, *Boundaries in Marriage* (Grand Rapids, MI: Zondervan, 1999), 9.

always protects, always trusts, always hopes, always perseveres. Love never fails." (1 Cor. 13:4-8a)

Paul clearly articulates what love is. Still, I have always found it helpful to paraphrase a text in my own words so it becomes personal. Here's my shot at it.

Love is longsuffering and tolerant. It is tender.

Love does not compare, nor does it stand for diminishing another's worth.

It does not offend others, as only seeking to meet one's own needs. Love does not get upset easily or quickly and will not keep a count of when it is offended. It does not enjoy being hurtful but instead joins joyfully in the truth. Love never stops providing safety, continues to believe the best, and perseveres. Love refuses to experience defeat.

Never is this more applicable than in times where there have been serious compromises of trust and extreme hurt done to one spouse or both. One thing love does not promise is that each person will be perfect. That said, while trust takes a long time to build, it takes an even longer time to rebuild.

One of my favorite television series is *Friends*. In a particular episode (Season 3, Episode 16, "The One the Morning After," 1997), two of the major characters, Ross and Rachel, have a complete breakdown in their relationship as a result of Ross making poor choices. After discovering how Ross broke this trust, Rachel says, *"You're a totally different person to me now. I used to think of you as somebody that would never, ever hurt me. Ever."*

I know most of us go into marriage never believing we will hurt the other or be subjected to disappointment by our spouse. Though I don't wish it upon any couple, I do want you to be prepared if it happens. Memorize and keep near the last part of those verses in 1st Corinthians 13 that we just talked about. Love always expects there to be sunshine after the rain. It always continues to work through the difficult times. Love never accepts anything less.

Can you imagine if your marriage modeled this kind of love in all areas? How productive, beneficial, and enjoyable a marriage it would be. Well, here is the great thing about this: IT CAN BE!

Conversations 2 Consider (C2C): Discuss-Ask-Act

1) Relive your wedding day.

2) What is something you know now about marriage that would have helped you tremendously if you knew when you first began your relationship with your spouse?

3) Read 1 Corinthians 13:4-8. Write what the words say to you.

14

A WIFE'S WORDS OF WISDOM

You may discover as you read these next few pages that I really love my husband. So when he asked me to write a chapter, I began brainstorming what I could say that he hadn't already said. I'll be honest, I'd rather read a book than contribute in writing one. Still, my love for my husband is what prompted me to participate. Besides hoping to share something new, I also wanted to make sure it would be of benefit to those reading.

I hope that as many men read this as do women. If you are a man, don't skip this chapter as I believe there will be some valuable information here for you, as well.

When William and I met in person for the first time, after weeks of talking on the phone, I knew right away that we would be something special. Maybe it was the way he looked or the way he looked at me. Maybe it was just the sun in my eyes. Whatever it was, it confirmed that what I felt, in our first phone conversation, would come to be.

It was 2001 and I was in the middle of watching *Dharma and Greg* when he called me. The show was about 10 minutes away from ending, so naturally I asked him (or rather told him) to call me back after the show was over. I really didn't think much of it then. However, when he called back 10 minutes later, I was completely shocked. Men don't do what they say they will, do they? William does. And I bet your husband strives to, as well.

I know that my husband, like yours, is busy and has a lot on his mind. So, if it takes longer for him to do something he said he would do, I am mindful not to mention that I am still waiting. Even if it doesn't materialize in the way or format expected, be careful not to devalue what he is working so hard to accomplish.

Just recently, a woman expressed vocally how much she would like to switch lives with me. Though I am sure she meant this to be a compliment to me and my husband, her spouse was standing right there when she said it. Can you imagine how he must have felt hearing his wife essentially wishing to trade what her husband has worked so hard for?

While not every reader is in the same situation, my husband is the breadwinner in our home. He works hard to provide. Whether he makes more or less, accomplishes what someone else does, or spends his time or our money the way another husband would, he cares for me the best way that he knows how.

If he were to overhear me being unappreciative of his effort, even without hurtful intentions, I believe it would crush him. I am grateful for all of his efforts. Therefore, I make sure never to compare him to another. My appreciation for him goes well beyond what he provides; rather my appreciation for him is rooted in *how hard* he works to provide.

I am certain I noticed this by watching my parents' marriage. My father was the primary income earner in our home. Though my mother worked outside the home for a time, she always reminded my dad of his value to our family. I can say that much of what I learned about marriage was due in large part to them.

Possibly the most valuable truth my mother impressed upon me was submission's value. Many women cringe hearing this word.

There is a misnomer that says when a woman submits, she is lowering herself or being a pushover.

However, that is not the case. Instead, my mother taught me that submission to her husband was God-honoring and assured him that he was loved and appreciated.

I've modeled my marriage after the great example they gave me. Even in the small things, I've willfully submitted. For example, a few years ago I had contemplated styling my hair a certain way. I shared on social media that I decided against doing so after my husband told me that he preferred that I didn't cut my hair.

Though I believed I was just sharing an innocent conversation, one individual stated that I should do whatever made me happy and not to allow my voice to be swallowed by my husband. She actually got pretty angry with me. I explained that he completely heard my voice, and while I had a choice, I chose not to go against his desire.

This wasn't an act of losing my say, but instead understanding what my husband liked, choosing to please him, and therefore expressing my love and appreciation of his input. In turn, he felt valued and heard. I trust him enough to know that he hears my voice, even when I don't speak.

The greatest benefit of submission to our husbands is that we are forcing ourselves to assume the best about them. We are confident our husbands have our interests at heart. We are trusting they are in communion with Christ daily and seeking to provide direction for our family. Submission shows that we trust them. With all our husbands are battling against, submission gives them confidence that there is someone in their corner with them.

One practical and physical way I can show my husband I am there with him is to actually be there for him. I am the first to congratulate him on an accomplishment. My ear is the first to open to hear a concern. I wait up late for him when he is gone and make sure he gets his goodnight kiss, even if that's all I can do before falling asleep. When he is out working late or getting a much needed Guys Night Out, I make sure he sees my face when he walks in the door.

That leads me to my final word of encouragement. Guys Night Out, for some, is almost as painful to hear as submitting. But you know what? I understand that when my husband goes to hang with the guys, it's not because he doesn't want to spend time with me. How do I know? Well, I assume the best, that's how. I assume he is spending time with the guys because he needs to have healthy interaction with other godly men. I know that he must spend some time not worried about the finances, the honey-do list, or the kids' schoolwork.

Your husband may not be one who likes a Guys Night Out. He may have other needs. Unless you ask him what it is that he needs, you won't know. Take the time and initiative to discover what he longs for. You may be surprised to find that some of what he yearns for are areas you desire as well.

Thanks babe for getting out of your comfort zone and writing what I believe are some critical truths to what has improved our marriage and can be of value to many others. —William

Conversations 2 Consider (C2C): Discuss-Ask-Act

1) Consider doubts you have had about your spouse at times and discuss them. Now assume the best regarding each doubt and discuss those.

2) Can you tell your spouse everything?

3) Sit and think about how hard your husband/wife works. Write down what you are especially grateful for and refer to this list often.

15

PILLOW TALK: IT'S NOT WHAT YOU THINK

Recently, I started a post on social media stating something to the point of how much I enjoyed the pillow talk my wife and I have at night. Within minutes of seeing and reading the post, my wife texted me and asked if I understood what "pillow talk" meant. I informed her that I was under the impression that the term referred to the innocent conversations a married couple has while laying down, but still awake. Imagine my shock when I discovered that was not what it meant.

However, this is expressly the meaning I want it to take over the first part of this chapter. The late night, half asleep, face to face, and even eyes closed conversations on our pillow have made a world of difference in our marriage. We've even committed to putting our phones and computers down every night from 8pm-10pm to make sure that we have some uninterrupted time to talk.

Just recently, we had a particularly difficult few nights walking through a tough conversation, working out some unresolved hurts and thoughts. Yet these nights, and many like it, have drawn us closer together. I am unsure if it is because our guards are down or because we strive not to go to bed with unsettled thoughts, but we've been able to be honest and move forward together as a result. I have discovered so much about my bride simply by taking 30 minutes at night talking to her about her day, her feelings, her dreams, and her tomorrow.

Many times, these minutes turn into hours of laughing, reminiscing, reflecting, and planning for our future. We may not have said a single word for a few minutes, when one or the other bursts out laughing, reminded of something earlier in the day. Other times we may just find ourselves jumping from one subject to another without any rhyme or reason.

This time, right before drifting off, is a good time to remind your spouse how important, valuable, and loved they are. Proverbs 16:24 reveals a vital truth about using this time:

Gracious words are a honeycomb, sweet to the soul and healing to the bones.

Make use of the time existing right before your eyes close. Tell your spouse something good about themselves. For as scripture assures, it will give sweet sleep to the soul and a restful night for the body.

That said, however, I want to address the common understanding of the title of this chapter. The conversations that happen before, after, or even instead of any physical encounter, are just as important, if not more than the physical act. Pillow talk is the flirty, sensual communication that creates a sense of anticipation and excitement between both spouses.

Naturally during this time, both partners are extremely near each other and likely to fall asleep close together or cuddling. According to a survey quoted in Women's Health magazine, the closer a husband and wife sleep, the stronger their bond is to each other.[11] In fact, it could even be said that pillow talk is a vital way for each partner to maintain their satisfaction and their closeness.

The closeness developed from pillow talk satisfies both a physical need and an emotional need. It draws each spouse closer, fulfilling the physical need by creating the pleasure and anticipation

---

[11] Kenny Thapoung, "6 Amazing Benefits of Cuddling," *Women's Health,* June 6, 2014, http://www.womenshealthmag.com/sex-and-love/benefits-of-cuddling/it-strengthens-your-bond.

of what is to come. Likewise, it allows each spouse to know they are engaged and involved, satisfying the much needed emotional demand as well.

Learning to use this time of talking and being close may be the most valuable lesson you take from this book. Use it to your advantage to make your marriage all the better. Allow these moments to be times where you find your safe haven, a rest from the doldrums of life, a fortress of peace from an unsettled world, and a place where you able to refill your emotional gas tank.[12]

Conversations 2 Consider (C2C): Discuss-Ask-Act

1) Discuss how pillow talk fulfills both your physical and emotional need.

2) Try it tonight. Take a few minutes, in the bed, just talking. Can you make time to do it most nights?

3) Find someone whose marriage has lasted longer than 30 years. Ask them what has been most critical to the length of their marriage.

---

[12] Samuel Raj, *Table Talk and Pillow Talk: A Guide to a Happier and Richer Life and Relationships* (Herndon, VA: Mascot Books, 2015), Kindle edition, Chapter 1.

16

TALK THEM UP

I hope no one reading this is guilty of the following, but I must be honest. There is nothing more insulting, infuriating, and annoying than hearing one spouse speaking about their partner in a negative manner. While it may not seem like it, doing so often reflects more of the innermost character of the spouse complaining rather than the shortcomings of the one who is the subject of the complaint.

If you are anything like me, you have high personal expectations and, at times, can become overly critical of yourself. Though I don't mean to, I catch myself too often putting myself down, saying words like, "*you messed up again,*" or "*William, you aren't smart for doing that.*" And while many books I've read, like *The Power of Positive Thinking* and *Awaken the Giant Within*, tell me how important it is to talk myself up, sometimes I just can't snap out of it.[13]   That said, hearing encouraging words are always welcomed. While many value the words of acquaintances, friends, and even extended family, hearing them from one's spouse is the *crème de la crème,* or the very best.

We, as spouses, do not have to use eloquent words or produce lengthy sentences for it to matter. Little notes, quick comments, short letters, small gestures, barely noticeable glances, and sensual touches are all ways to let your spouse know how much they mean to you. While it is certainly valuable in private, find ways to praise your spouse in public.

Now, I know you may be reading this, saying to yourself, *"Ugh, it is annoying to see husbands and wives gush over each other."* Well guess what? It may be. You are not doing it for them anyway. Surely, your spouse will not mind. In fact, they may return the favor the next time someone asks them about you.

When I overhear Kelly telling someone how proud she is of me or how well I treat her, it makes me swell with joy and encourages me to find even more ways to create that feeling of pride that she has in me. I want to continue to give her reasons to talk favorably of me. And you know what? I think she wants just as

---

[13] Norman Peale, *The Power of Positive Thinking,* (NYC: Fireside, 1952) and Tony Norman, *Awaken the Giant Within,* (New York City, NY: Free Press, 1991).

much to be able to tell others how highly she looks at me. Selfishly, publicly praising your partner is bound to benefit you.

There is a second meaning to talking your spouse up as well. Talk them up to your Heavenly Father. Pray for them constantly. Pray for the tangible things (i.e. their health, careers, safety, etc.). Pray for the intangible areas (i.e. their choices, mentality, passions, etc.).

One of God's purposes in marriage is to shape us to be more like Him. He accomplishes drawing us closer to Him by connecting us to another who rubs down the jagged edges of our hearts and sands down the callous spots in our lives. My spouse has taken on the responsibility of doing this difficult work as we walk to the cross every day of our marriage. I promise you, this is not easy, but the resulting closeness we have with each other and with our Creator, is worth it.

This prayer to God and proclamation to others reveals the heart of talking our spouses up. Husbands, as we lead our brides to the cross daily, we are talking with the Creator about what she needs, to be the wife we know she longs to be. Wives, as you follow your husbands to the cross, you can talk to God about the joy you possess in being joined to a husband who leads you there.

Going before God on behalf of our spouse is one of the greatest privileges of our marriage. It takes the tendency of placing ourselves as the top priority and replaces it with elevating our spouse's needs in the superior spot. A great part of this privilege is expressly knowing that our partners are praying for us as well and then watching God move in response to our prayers.

Conversations 2 Consider (C2C): Discuss-Ask-Act

1) Discuss what your spouse does that makes you appreciate them.

2) What are you saying about your spouse to others?

3) Put a note on the fridge or in their lunch or in their vehicle's cup holder tomorrow morning.

4) Set an alarm to talk your spouse up to God each day until the alarm is no longer needed.

17

IDEAS

The following represent a small list of ideas for intentionally spending time with your spouse:

1. Catch a drive in movie.

2. Mold some pottery.

3. Create a painting.

4. Drive through your dream neighborhood.

5. Go fishing.

6. Rent a kayak.

7. Get a hotel for the weekend.

8. Pack a picnic.

9. Sign up for a dance class.

10. Take a wine tour.

11. Paint a room an odd color.

12. Go indoor rock climbing.

13. Test drive your dream car.

14. Embark on a scavenger hunt.

15. Hike a trail.

16. Get lost.

17. Escape a mirror maze.

18. Visit a historic landmark.

19. Volunteer together.

20. Window shop.

21. People watch on a park bench.

22. Visit a dinner theatre.

23. Do a puzzle.

24. Fly a kite.

25. Go camping.

26. Ride a tandem bike.

27. See a play.

28. Catch a fish.

29. Share a sundae.

30. Find the constellations.

31. Make out in the back of the library.

32. Visit a museum.

33. Go to the fair.

34. Write a short story.

35. Put your phones down and talk.

36. Work out.

37. Feed the ducks.

38. Talk with residents of a nursing home.

39. Renew your vows.

40. Walk hand in hand.

41. Meet your neighbors.

42. Try new food.

43. Discover your ancestry.

44. Play Truth or Dare.

45. Visit an art gallery.

46. Watch the sunset.

47. Complete and obstacle course.

48. Watch the sunrise.

49. Give gifts on a day other than Christmas or birthdays.

50. Sign up for a cooking class.

51. Wake up and go for a jog.

52. Take a cruise.

53. Build something for the house.

54. Tailgate.

55. Go bird watching.

56. Couples pedicure.

57. Find a pumpkin at a local pumpkin patch.

58. Ride public transportation.

59. Catch a concert.

60. Pick fresh fruit.

Conversations 2 Consider (C2C): Discuss-Ask-Act

1) Once you've read these ideas, discuss some of the potential suggestions you could try.

2) What else can you think of that is not listed?

3) Circle at least 5. Put together a plan that allows you to do them this month. They don't have to be big ones. They don't have to be all in one day, or they can be. All that matters is that you do them.

18

WRAPPING UP

Your marriage is important:

- it is important to God as He is its creator

- it is important to you and your spouse as you two are the committed

- it is important to your children as they are the product of your union and will model their lives after yours

Here are some final truths, though potentially deserving of their own separate chapters, I've decided just to leave as one liners.

- Work together on common dreams, but prioritize each other more than those dreams.

- Opposites may attract, but likeminded people experience longer and more enjoyable marriages.

- Going to bed angry won't harm your marriage as much as waking up the next morning just as mad will.

- Realize it usually isn't your spouse that has changed, but rather your perception that has.

- Holding hands and gentle kisses on the cheek can go a long way.

Crystal Sullivan, editor of Family Ministries in Chicago says it best. *"Marriages that last a lifetime don't just happen; they are built one day at a time, as we make decisions to love our spouses. We stand at the altar and promise to God and the community that we will love each other in good times and in bad, not knowing how much good or how much bad will come our way."*[14]

There is no magic to marriage, however you have the choice to make it magical.

---

[14] Rob Scuka, "Marriages That Last a Lifetime," *Family Ministries,* edited by Crystal Sullivan (April 2007), accessed June 14, 2016, https://www.familyministries.org/newsletter.asp?newsletter_id=13.

ABOUT THE AUTHOR

William Thomas has been married to his wife Kelly for over 15 years. They married as teenagers and began a family about a year and a half later. William joined the United States Navy prior to 9/11 and served four years afterwards, until being medically discharged.

They now have four children, Madison, Mackenzie, Macey, and William Phillip II. They currently homeschool and reside in north Georgia. William possesses an undergraduate degree in Religion from Liberty University, as well as his Master of Arts in Christian Ministries from the same institution.

William, Kelly, and their children enjoy traveling the country in their RV and have been to every state in America save Hawaii and Alaska. The greatest joy of traveling is seeing their children gain new experiences and make lasting memories. They are both actively serving in their church and love to spend time with their extended families. William enjoys public speaking, ministering, and encouraging others to strive towards their full potential.

Kelly enjoys decorating their home for each holiday, cross-stitching, reading, and talking about the future with William.

While William enjoys writing, this is his first published work.

HOW TO CONTACT

Feel free to send an email to William at thought2text@yahoo.com

Connect with us on Facebook-"It's Not Magic: But It Can Be Magical."

Feel free to write a letter to P.O. Box 356 Woodstock, GA 30188 with a return address clearly written on the front of the envelope.

IT'S NOT MAGIC